Dowey Lad Goes to Sea
In the Fifties

Derek Dowey

Dowey Lad Goes to Sea
In the Fifties

Derek Dowey

Cover photo ©Fotoflite of Ashford

ISBN 9781912821983

A CIP catalogue record for this book is available from the British Library

Published 2021 Tricorn Books
131 High Street, Portsmouth,
PO1 2HW

Printed & bound in the UK

Dowey Lad Goes to Sea
In the Fifties

For
my lovely Alison

Dowey Lad Goes to Sea
In the Fifties

I was born into a military family in India in 1940 and we travelled by troopship to several places in the old Empire. By the time Dad was posted to Hong Kong in 1954 I was already in love with the sea and ships and Hong Kong confirmed my love. All sorts and sizes of vessels used the harbour and the way to see them was to take a trip on the Star Ferry which links the island of Hong Kong with the Kowloon mainland. Ocean liners tied up on the Kowloon-side right beside the Star Ferry terminal. It was possible to go on board providing you had a pass from a shipping company office so, together with some friends, I would visit some of the ocean liners. Our favourites were the British P&O liners (*Chusan, Canton and Corfu*) and the French Messageries Maritimes vessels (*Laos* and *Cambodia*). They were splendid. Now how about the Merchant Navy as a career? Well yes, I believed I would enjoy that but, in early 1957, as we left Hong Kong to return to the UK on the British India liner *Nevasa* the plan was for me to finish my school studies in Northern Ireland and then take the Sandhurst military academy entrance exam.

As I settled into my new school I continued to think about what to do in life. Was it to be the Army or would I prefer the Merchant Navy? Eventually I wrote to Dad who was serving in a military post in Ghana and told him that I had decided to go to sea. He replied very positively and said I should go where I felt I would be happiest. Letters went off to seven shipping companies offering my services as a Navigation Cadet. (They were all reputable companies and their worldwide routes looked interesting.) I received six replies: one said sorry but that I needed A Level certificates, however the other five called me forward for interview. Clan Line Steamers was the pick of the bunch; it had a very good reputation and fine sea routes so I declined the others. I explained to Clan Line that I had another week to complete the school term and then I could go over for interview. Their reply was that I should go to the Board of Trade medical centre in Belfast for a physical check-up. If I passed (and was given a certificate) they would accept me unseen. A uniform list was included. I was to telephone them at their HQ in the Royal Liver Building in Liverpool to discuss when I would be able to report there. They would then assign me to a ship. (Liverpool was their main UK port together with Birkenhead just across the Mersey.) *Blimey! This is happening fast! I'd better get a move on!*

Several shipping companies shared the Liver Building on the waterfront. It has two mythical bird statues on each of its twin towers. Apparently they are a mixture of eagle and cormorant. There are several legends about the birds. One says that the birds will only flap their wings when a lady of untarnished reputation passes by. Hmmmm. And goes on to say that nobody has ever seen the wings flap. Anyway, I reported to the Clan Line offices in the building.

"Ah yes. Cadet Dowey. Welcome aboard... so to speak. If you could take a seat at that table, there are some forms we would like you to complete. Your ship, the *Clan Macleod*, is due here in three days time. In the meantime, you need to report to *Clan Cameron* for accommodation and food. She is in the Alexandra Dock."

So, after some form-filling, that's where I went.

Cargo ships in harbour are not usually the nicest places to be. *Clan Cameron* was no exception. She was a 20 year-old cargo ship of just over 7,000 tons deadweight and was beginning to show her age. (In fact, she was scrapped two years later.) She would have looked fine at sea with everything shipshape but in harbour she was a mess: repairs going on, gangs of men hammering and banging everywhere, cargo being loaded/unloaded. However I was given a cabin and my meals and generally left in peace. One evening I took a bus into the city to see a film. It was *Frankenstein*. It scared the wits out of me; I had nightmares for some time after that. After the show, a chap came up to me as I waited for a bus back to the docks.

"Hello there. What ship are you on?"

"I'll be on the *Clan Macleod* but she isn't in yet."

"Well that's a coincidence, I'll be joining her as the relief Carpenter while she's in home waters. So I'll be seeing you on board shortly."

"That's good. But here's my bus."

"Just before you go, you couldn't lend me, say, ten shillings until I see you?"

"Well, sorry. I've got just enough for my bus fare."

"Oh, too bad."

Off he went and I hopped on my bus. He never appeared on the *Macleod*. A con man.

After a couple of days I was told that my ship had docked in Birkenhead and that I should join her. I found her in Vittoria Dock which Clan Line shared with the Blue Funnel Line (Holts). The *Macleod's* permanent crewmen were on board – mainly Indians from the Bombay area – but the officers were all stand-ins while the deep-sea officers took their leave. Soon I was to love the *Clan Macleod* but she was not looking her best in the teeming rain and with shore crews doing all sorts of work on deck. She had been built on the Clyde in 1948 and was over 6,000 tons deadweight. Her 'laid-back' appearance was due to having three large cargo holds forward of the main superstructure and two small ones aft. Her black and white colours were smart, and the black funnel had the traditional two red hoops of the Clan Line. When shipshape and sailing she was one of the smartest little ships you could hope to see. In fact, she adorns the cover of the book about the Clan Line, *Gathering of the Clans* by Norman Middlemiss. I was shown to my cabin which was much better than I had expected. It had three bunk beds with fitted drawers, a writing desk, chair, three wardrobes and a basin. A small adjacent cabin was equipped as a study. Not many shipping lines provided the cadets with their own Cabin Steward but Clan Line did, although he also worked in the galley and dining room.

The first few days were difficult for me being the only cadet on board at the time. I was brand new, hadn't been to cadet school and consequently knew nothing. I had to learn fast. The stand-in Third Mate gave me a note and told me to go down to the Storeman and bring back a certain item. The Storeman gave me a large ball of thick string and I set off to find the Third Mate. As I made my way along one of the corridors (the inside of the ship was a sort of ants' nest of corridors and gangways) I was accosted by the stand-in First Mate:

"What's that you've got, Dowey lad?" (I was always 'Dowey lad' to my seniors during my time at sea.)

"It's a ball of twine for the Third Mate, sir."

"A ball of twine, Dowey lad?! A ball of twine?! That's boat-lacing, Dowey lad. We don't use twine at sea! Housewives use twine in kitchens!"

"Yes sir! Boat-lacing it is, sir!"

"And don't you forget it, Dowey lad! Ball of twine indeed!"

I realised that I would have to spend a good part of my off-duty time with my nose in my sea manuals and also talking to the old Sea Dogs. Later:

"Dowey lad. Get a couple of clusters down in Number Two hold tween-decks."

"Aye aye, sir!"

I didn't understand what the hell he was talking about, so I went off to find someone who did. I was told that one of the tasks which cadets performed was to arrange the lighting in cargo holds. Some holds had their own lighting system but others required 'clusters'; these were arrays of light bulbs on a sort of shield with a long length of flex. You rigged them up in dark parts of the holds so that the dockers could do their work. Bulbs were continually blowing and forever needed replacing.

We were to be in Birkenhead for only a couple more days before sailing for Glasgow. Meantime, I formally 'signed on' in the presence of the stand-in Captain and the Purser. Signing the ship's articles is an ancient and necessary procedure. They set out pay and other benefits, treatment that one could expect and penalties for infractions. I was to be paid £2 a week with free food and, of course, free accommodation.

"Let go for'ard" and then "Let go aft" and we eased away from Birkenhead docks. Then out into the Mersey and up the estuary to the Irish Sea. I was on the bridge writing up the log and also acting as lookout.

"Dowey lad. Find the Chief Engineer, give him my compliments and ask him if he would kindly join me in my cabin at 18.00."

"Compliments to the Chief Engineer, kindly see Captain in his cabin at 18.00 it is sir." (I was learning fast!)

And off I went. I hunted high and low but couldn't find him. Later:

"Can't find the Chief Engineer, sir."

"Oh really, Dowey lad. Do you suppose he's gone for a swim?"

Hoots of laughter all round the bridge.

"Never mind, Dowey lad. Never mind."

I don't know if the whole thing had been a joke being played on the new cadet. Perhaps the Chief Engineer had hidden himself away. But jokes were often played on new cadets. I was told later of an incident on another ship a couple of years earlier. It went like this:

Captain: "Lad, my compliments to the Chief Engineer who is in the engine room just now. Ask him for the key of the keelson and then you bring it up here. Tell him we'll return it to him shortly."

Cadet: "Key of the keelson from the Chief Engineer it is sir!'

And off he went.

11

Chief Engineer: "Ahh. It's the key of the keelson you're after is it? Well, I saw it a short time ago. Ah, yes. There it is over in the corner."

And the Chief went across and dragged out a large pipe of irregular shape with various metal brackets on it.

Chief Engineer: "Here it is lad. My compliments to the Captain and inform him that I would like it back by 18.00."

Cadet: "I will sir."

So the cadet lugged the heavy, unwieldy pipe up the ladders from the engine room and then on up a couple of companion-ways to the bridge.

"Key of the keelson, sir. The Chief Engineer would like it back by 18.00."

All those on the bridge were in hysterics. There is no such thing as a 'key of the keelson'. The hot, sweaty new cadet was not amused. He picked up the tangle of metal he had been given and hurled it overboard.

Shrieks from all on the bridge... but too late. It was gone.

It turned out that the pipe was an important engine room item and was due to be refitted that evening. Too bad.

Our voyage to Glasgow was uneventful but memorable. I was on the bridge as the *Macleod* turned into the Clyde. As dawn broke on this clear summer morning it revealed the islands and the inlets of the

Clyde estuary; I had never seen a more beautiful vista... and still haven't. Pinks then reds and golds as the sun came up, followed by greens and blues. The sea as calm as a village pond. Wonderful. However, the port and shipbuilding yards of our destination – Govan – could not in any way be described as beautiful; Govan was simply an industrial outpost of Glasgow. The *Macleod* was returning to near her birthplace (Clan Line had its own shipbuilding yard) and immediately went into dry dock for periodic servicing. Dry-docking was quite a performance but the newest cadet in the British Merchant Marine had little to do:

"Just observe and learn, Dowey lad."

"Yes, sir."

We were in dry dock for a week and the ship was in a right old noisy mess for much of the time, with teams of shore workmen doing all sorts of servicing things; others banged away on the hull underneath and the propeller was removed, serviced and replaced.

One of my jobs in dry dock was to go ashore each morning to buy newspapers for the Navigating Officers – the posh lot on the ship. (The Engineer Officers must have made their own arrangements.) The trouble was that I couldn't understand the strong Glasgow dialect, so in the newsagents I simply pointed and paid over the money. On the first morning, the nearest newsagent stocked only *The Daily Worker* so I bought four of them. I had never come across this paper before (remember, I had spent most of my life so far as a colonial) but assumed it was a local Glasgow one. When I got back to the ship and distributed the copies to the Captain, First, Second and Third Mates each said more or less the same thing:

"Dowey lad, why the hell did you buy this Communist rubbish for me?!"

Oh yes, Govan was quite red in those days. On future mornings I had to go further afield to find 'proper' newspapers.

There was a pressing need for me to go into Glasgow city. I had joined the *MacLeod* in my smart doe-skin uniform thinking that they would provide me with working clothes to do all the dirty work that a cadet has to do.

"No, Dowey lad. Not so. You must kit yourself out with your own working clothes. Good gracious lad, we give you everything else, don't we? Board and lodgings, your shared cabin servant, free travel around the world, a girl in every port, etc. So you get yourself up to Glasgow. Go to Millets shop; they always have second-hand boiler suits and denims and things."

So I drew my credits from the Purser. After some deductions it amounted to three shillings and sixpence. The tram fare was three pence each way, leaving three shillings to buy some working clothes. I found Millets and went straight to the rack of second-hand boiler suits. Having the build of the sort of chap who gets sand kicked in his face on the beach, none of the boiler suits fitted me. So I bought the least voluminous. It cost three shillings but they must have felt sorry for me as they threw in an old belt and a well-worn blue beret that had been lying around. Then back to the ship with my treasures. Now all I needed was an old pair of shoes. I consulted my Cabin Steward who said that a previous cadet had left an old pair of shoes in one of the cupboards. They were too big for me but I managed to slop around in them. Now I was properly equipped for the scraping, painting and oiling jobs which fill a large part of a Navigation Cadet's day.

Before we left Govan we loaded some crates of alcohol destined for South Africa. I was assigned to the special lock-up area in one of the lower holds to supervise the safe stowage of the crates. The Mates warned me that the Glasgow dockers were smart and would steal as much liquor as they could. And sure enough, they did. Even though I was keeping a sharp eye on the loading of the crates, the dockers were becoming quite merry. So before the next net-full of crates was slung over from the dock, I locked up the special area and raced up ladders to report to the Mate. On my way up I saw the evidence of what was happening – empty bottles. One of the dockers had stationed himself at a higher level and, as a sling came down the crane man would slow it so that a crate could be removed. The 'Bar Man' would then take the crate over to a dark corner and his mates would visit from time to time for a few gulps of good Scotch whisky. Anyway, on up to see the Mate.

"Only to be expected, Dowey lad. Some of them would rob their own grandmother of her last sixpence. I'll send the Third Mate down with you to stop that nonsense."

Shortly before we sailed, another brand new cadet joined. Bob was a Scot from Kirkcudbright who had been to Leith Cadet School. So he knew much, much more about our job than I did. But I had been to sea (well, a wee bit of the sea) and had stood lookout on the bridge so that evened things up a little; and I knew my way around the *Macleod* and what was expected of us. Bob was a nice enough chap but he talked and talked and talked. Within a couple of days I knew his life story and those of his entire family.

Eventually the *Macleod* was ready for sea again, so we took on our Clyde Pilot and headed down river. Our next port was to be Middlesbrough so as soon as we hit the open sea we sailed north between the west coast of Scotland and the outlying islands. The weather was perfect: warm and sunny with hardly a breath of wind. The sea was flat calm and the scenery terrific: the islands and the coast were so clearly defined. The flat calm meant that any sea life breaking the surface was easy to spot; we were fortunate to come across several basking sharks grazing lazily on plankton at the surface of the sea. These sharks can be up to 11 metres in length. Then, at the top of Scotland, we turned hard right (or, as I now knew it to be *hard-astarb'd*) at Cape Wrath and headed east into the Pentland Firth. This separates the north of Scotland from the Orkney Islands. There can be a terrific tidal race in the Pentland. We had to plough slowly eastwards against a ten knot current. As the *Macleod* could make only 14 knots, it was a slow journey along the top of Scotland. Bob and I were now on 'watch about' on the bridge – four hours on and four off. Then we were told that 'Dog Watches' would be done that evening. So, we split the 16.00 to 20.00 watch into two of two hours each. This changes the cycle of four-hour watches if you are on 'watch about' for several days.

At last we reached Middlesbrough where the third cadet, Ian, rejoined the ship after leave. He had been on its previous voyage and had two years' sea service. Middlesbrough is unlikely to be on anyone's 'must visit' list, and I remember only two things about it. In my attempt to become a Sea Dog as quickly as possible I decided I needed a pipe. Besides, Dad smoked one and he loved it. So I collected a few more shillings from the Purser and set off to buy one. It didn't take long as there wasn't a wide selection in my price range. I bought a smart brown curvy one – a kind of mini Sherlock Holmes type. But I didn't have enough money left for tobacco. That would have to wait until I had earned some more cash. The other memory of Middlesbrough was the loading of iron railway lines for South Africa. How do you get railway lines into the holds of ships? Well, you need skilled dockers, and Middlesbrough certainly had them. The shore dockers prepared a rail, the winchman on the ship hoisted it from the dockside and swung it over an open hatch. A couple of dockers then manoeuvred it into position at a tilt, and then down the rail went. Then came the really tricky bit... but it was over in seconds: while the rail was still dangling, dockers in the lower hold pulled it into the storage position and it dropped down snugly, face up. When they had carpeted the hold with a single layer of rails face up, down came the next batch. These came face down meaning that when they were dropped into place they fitted perfectly into the first layer of rails. It was all done very quickly and seemingly with great ease. The Middlesbrough dockers were real professionals and the best I came across. We were now loading seriously for our voyage to South Africa but there was more cargo to collect on the continent. Our next port of call was to be Hamburg on the Elbe.

After an uneventful voyage across one of the most

boring seas in the world – the North Sea, looking like oxtail soup – we picked up our Pilot at the mouth of the Elbe River and he took us upstream to Hamburg. In any congested area (rivers, canals or going into harbour or leaving), the main duty of the cadet on the bridge was to record in the logbook virtually anything that happened and the time. In particular, the time of passing buoys, light-ships, headlands and other ships. So that is what I did, with little time for watching the passing countryside. As for Hamburg itself, I can remember little about what went on there in the ship. I have no memory of the cargo we unloaded and loaded. But what I can remember is rushing off to visit the Reeperbahn with Bob. The street called Reeperbahn was (is?) famous for its prostitutes. We wandered along goggle-eyed at the displays. The ladies were sitting virtually naked behind glass. They were, in fact, sitting in shop fronts waiting for clients. Even if we had had the nerve to knock on a door (which we didn't), we didn't have enough money. Instead, we bought some popcorn and munched it thoughtfully as we made our way back to the *Macleod*. Soon we sailed again, this time heading for Rotterdam and Antwerp.

Rotterdam on the Rhine estuary was a huge port but we were only in for a short time before we were on our way again. However, in Antwerp there was a lot to load so we were there for a couple of days. Limited shore leave was granted. The Purser gave me my wages and I went ashore with Jim, the Second

Radio Officer ('Second Sparks'), a young chap in his twenties. Having heard about Belgium's reputation for good food, we decided that the first thing to do was to have a good steak. As we sat at a pavement table on a lovely summer's day we agreed that this was the life – being paid to sail around the world and visit interesting places. The menu showed that a steak was within my budget. It duly appeared but with nothing else.

"Don't we get any vegetables with the steak?"

"Yes you do, if you order them and pay for them."

The lonely steak was excellent.

But the real reason for going ashore was to buy tobacco for my pipe. I had already christened it with tobacco someone had given me but needed my own stock for the long voyage to southern Africa. Those who knew about these things had advised that Antwerp was the place to buy tobacco at a good price. So, off to a tobacconist to be confronted with a bewildering display of packets of all sorts. Eventually I chose one based on attractive packaging and a price I could afford. Then back to the ship to get on with some serious pipe smoking. This was not successful. After a few puffs I was practically choking. However, I reasoned that if I kept at it through short sessions I would soon get used to pipe smoking and become a real Sea Dog.

By now the *Macleod* was fully loaded with a mixed cargo for southern African ports – rail lines, machinery of various sorts, European liquor, cars, etc. Some of the Indian crew had also been accumulating their own private 'cargo' – old clothes. They had a patient scheme with a good final pay-off. It started with buying old clothes in the so-called 'Home Ports' (British and North West European) with the intention of selling them in Africa. Then they would hold on to that money until their next trip to Indian ports – that could be next year or in three or four years' time. It didn't matter; they were patient. In India, they would buy gold. Once back in UK they would sell the gold and then buy presents and household goods for their families in India and, of course, another pile of second-hand clothes. And so the cycle would continue. Most of the crew were very careful with their money and put most of it to use in this ingenious and patient cycle of purchases and sales. In some cases, a large extended family (perhaps even a small village) back in India was relying on the efforts of a single seaman.

It was now time to clear away from the Home Ports and to head south. We had business with four South African ports and two in Portuguese East Africa. First of all there was the English Channel to contend with; in those days it was the busiest seaway in the world. The three Navigation Cadets stood watches with the Mates on the bridge while the Captain spent much of his time stalking it, getting in the way and disappearing for a catnap now and again. In addition to this state of vigilance, we had a member of the crew right up on the bow as lookout. When he spotted a ship/light he signalled with the for'ard bell: one ring for ship/light to starb'd, two to port and three for straight ahead. Having cleared the cluttered Channel we then faced the Bay of Biscay. It's probably calm sometimes but I have never found it to be so. This time it was thoroughly unpleasant: rough with rain and strong winds coming in from the west. The sea-lanes through the Bay are very busy so the cadets, with their young keen eyes, continued doing watches on the bridge and maintaining the logbook.

At last we were clear of the heavy traffic and headed for southern Africa. Thankfully it was now time for normal shipboard routine. On the navigating side, the three Mates split 24 hours into six watches. I thought that the Third Mate being the junior would have the worst watches but no, he had the best: 08.00–12.00 and 20.00–24.00. It was the Second Mate who drew the short straw: 12.00–16.00 and then the 'graveyard' watch midnight–04.00. The Chief Mate took the 16.00–20.00 and 04.00–08.00; doing the early morning stint made sense as, towards the end of the watch, senior crew members would come up to be briefed on the working day ahead. The Senior Cadet would also report to him to get our orders for the day. The Captain's tasks? He did whatever was necessary for the smooth running of the ship but he didn't stand watches unless one of the Mates was ill. And our tasks? Well, the idea was that in our four years as cadets we would learn as much about work and life on a ship as possible. If we didn't, we would fail the Ministry of Transport exam to qualify as a Mate. So we were involved in near-shore and deep sea navigation of course, plus cargo duties, ship maintenance, etc. The object was for us to be able eventually to do virtually every job that the deck crew had to do, but also, of course, to be capable of carrying out a Third Mate's tasks. Our chief mentor for all of this was the Chief Mate but we also learnt from the other officers.

One particular recurring job could be rather dangerous. The Duty Cadet would have to test the temperatures of the cargo holds both at mid-morning and mid-afternoon. He equipped himself with a very large thermometer attached to a long hank of boat-lacing. Then he would walk along the open deck and lift a metal flap above each hold (we had five) and dangle the thermometer down a pipe into the holds. It was left there for at least ten minutes so that the thermometer could register the true temperature. Of course, the reason for this exercise was in case of fire and it acknowledged the possibility of spontaneous combustion of certain kinds of cargo. Without these frequent checks, the ship could be sailing along apparently serenely but with a smouldering fire building up in a hold. Our temperature-checking job was hardly intellectually taxing but, if the ship was running through heavy seas, it was quite dangerous. Indeed sometimes very dangerous. At times, ropes had to be rigged for hand-holds, and more than one man could be required for the temperature-checking: one trying to do the testing and the other holding on to him with one arm, with the other hanging on for dear life to the rail or rope. In heavy seas and rain you couldn't avoid returning to your cabin sopping wet in spite of your oil-skins... and not a little frightened. But the job had to be done, without fail.

Perhaps the worst job we had was chipping the open decks which were bare steel. Steel rusts particularly well when drenched in salt water. We would set to with the crew armed with hammers and chip the rust off. If the weather was good we would wear only shoes and shorts and perhaps a beret. What was the point of getting our clothes covered in red rust dust? Better to do it virtually bare and have a good shower later. So there we were with goggles protecting our eyes, covered in rust dust, hammering away and cursing. Most of our other tasks were pretty dirty. I never managed to get rid of all the paint on my hands until the end of a trip; on board, you would just about get cleaned up and then you would be given another dirty job. And at meal times the cadets would be wolfing down their food displaying technicolour hands. Also our clothes got grimy, of course. Every couple of days the drill was to dunk your latest lot of dirty clothes into a large bucket of water, add some soap powder and leave it overnight. Then, during your next shower (in the tropics we needed salt-water showers two or three times a day), you would chuck the clothes on the shower floor and mark time on them while showering. Quite effective. Sometimes, if we were using white paint, we would disguise ourselves as Jeff Chandler, the film star. He was well known for the grey hair on the sides of his head and ladies quite liked that – or so we were told. So, if we were using white paint, we would brush some on the sides of our heads before going down to lunch. The officers were used to this by now and there would be groans:

"Oh no. Here come the Jeff Chandlers."

For most of our voyage south, the Atlantic was calm and there was hardly any wind so we made good time. The weather was grand and the sea lanes uncrowded. Most people were in good spirits and enjoying the routine of a well-run ship. However, relations between the three cadets could have been better. Bob was an easy-going chap and I got on well with him; he and Ian were friends also. But there was a problem between Ian and me. He was the senior with two years' experience but instead of simply leading us he seemed to want to dominate us. I wasn't having that. When things went wrong he tended to blame me. One morning, Ian came back from his meeting with the First Mate with a list of jobs for the day. Bob and I were assigned work on the 'Flying Bridge'. This was a platform on top of the normal bridge. It had duplicate steering gear, engine room signal equipment and navigating instruments. It was useful for Navigators at times when they needed more height to see ahead, and was a back-up bridge when there were problems on the main bridge. However, it was hardly ever used apart from Morse lamp-signalling by the cadets. For that we would go up there with the Chief Mate to be put through our Morse paces. If there was a passing ship we would sometimes try to call it up. They would quickly see that we were a bunch of 'makey-learnies' and would either ignore us or patiently reply to our laborious practice signals. But back to the job in hand; the Flying Bridge needed maintenance so Bob and I had a scraping and painting job to do. Bob went off to get the paint and I collected some scrapers and cloths and things. We were in good form, chatting and singing and well into our work when Ian appeared. Something had happened which had been brought to his attention. Ian addressed me:

"A pot of paint has been knocked over in the paint store but the mess wasn't cleaned up properly. The Storekeeper has complained to the Chief Mate about it and said that it must have been one of the cadets as we are the only other people who have access to his stores."

Well, it wasn't me; I hadn't been in the paint store for a couple of days. I carried on painting. Bob said nothing.

"Derek, I'm speaking to you."

"Fine, I heard you."

"What do you know about it?"

I continued to paint. Bob said nothing.

"I want an answer from you."

"My answer is that I don't like being spoken to in this way."

Bob said nothing.

"I shall need to report this to the Chief Mate."

"Go ahead. If he wants to talk to me he will call for me."

Bob said nothing. Ian stalked off. I turned towards Bob but he wouldn't look at me. I never heard any more about the spilt paint but this was an example of the sort of relationship I had with Ian. It wasn't good, especially as we three shared a cabin.

At sea, cadets worked from 07.00 to 17.00 with time off, of course, for breakfast, lunch and a short tea break. We were supposed to study in the evenings and each of us had a heavy set of nautical books to help us towards eventually passing the Second Mate's exam (there was no Third Mate's exam). Cadets on Clan Line ships were fortunate as we had an Indian crew, often called a Lascar crew (the term is Urdu and means native military or naval personnel). On ships with a British crew, cadets were often treated virtually as deckhands, whereas in the Clan Line we were thought of as junior (very junior!) officers. It was said that for every British seaman you would need two Lascars. (It was also said that a Chinese seaman was twice as good as his British counterpart!) We used Indian words for the Lascar appointments. The top man was the Bosun who we called 'Serang'; the Bosun's Mate was 'Tindal'; 'Secuni' was the name for Quartermaster; a Storeman was 'Casab'. They called the Captain 'Captain Sahib', and the Chief Mate 'Burra Malim Sahib' which translates, appropriately, as 'Big Know-Everything Boss'. And, in the case of the *Macleod's* Chief Mate, that was absolutely right. The great thing about having an Indian crew was that we had Indian chefs. And they could certainly cook. Apart from normal 'British' fare, a curry dish was also available at lunchtime. The chefs had a large repertoire and you would certainly not have the same variety of curry coming round within a fortnight. As cadets, we ate everything available. Thus we tucked in to both the 'normal' main course and the curry alternative: four courses – soup, curry, main course, pudding. We were usually on the first sitting (of two) for lunch and should have been out after half an hour. However, we asked for an extra 15 minutes into the second sitting so that we could give appropriate attention to our meals. The Chief Mate called us disgusting brutes but agreed to our request.

But let's continue the journey down the South Atlantic. We were still painting the Flying Bridge when I glanced ahead and thought I saw something on the surface of the sea and directly in line with the ship's course. Something seemed to be waving. I raced down to the bridge and pointed it out to the Mate on duty. Through our binoculars it looked like a man in the water waving an arm. Blimey! Way out in the South Atlantic there's a man in the water! The Mate was about to order 'Slow Down' to the engine room when, as we got closer, we saw what it was – a seal, floating on its back with one flipper flapping lazily to and fro across its chest. It wasn't in the least disturbed by the presence of a ship bearing down on it. In fact it manoeuvred slightly so that it could watch us pass about fifty yards away. It rocked up and down on our bow waves, observing us and seemingly waving us on our way with one of its flippers.

Our first port of call in South Africa was to be Cape Town. The Old Hands said it was a super place and we looked forward to it eagerly. There are some ports so scenic that they almost take your breath away as you sail in. Cape Town is one. Everybody (apart from engine room staff) was on deck as we took on our Pilot and eased our way slowly into Table Bay.

Sailing into harbour, the Navigators were distributed like this:

- On the bridge, the Captain and Pilot plus the Third Mate. Also the Junior Cadet logging everything that happened.
- For'ard, the Chief Mate with the Senior Cadet.
- Aft, the Second Mate and the other cadet.

Bob and I took turns during the voyage at being 'the Junior Cadet' and I was on the bridge for Cape Town. It was the best place to be. The town itself looked lovely with its magnificent backdrop of Table Mountain. But there was bad news: no waiting for a berth and no shore leave. We went straight in, docked, unloaded a small amount of cargo (mainly the remaining crates of whisky from Glasgow!) and were on our way within a couple of hours.

"Never mind, Dowey lad. In your time with Clan Line you'll have plenty of other opportunities to see Cape Town. And tomorrow we'll be in Port Elizabeth. You'll get a run ashore there."

Just south of Cape Town is the Agulhas Bank, a long shallow feature where the warm Indian Ocean currents meet their cold Atlantic cousins. Sailing across the Bank can be very uncomfortable, with reputedly the biggest sea swells in the world. If you are prone to seasickness you will suffer. We were really pleased when we were through it.

Between ports there was plenty to do. Sometimes we were lent to the Carpenter ('Chippy') to do various tasks. If a hold had been cleared of cargo we would go down to clean up generally but also to inspect the 'dunnage'. Dunnage was a term used to describe anything which protected cargo – sheets of plastic, matting of various sorts and, especially, wooden planks. On our ship, we used the latter only. Strips of dunnage would be laid on the metal decks in holds with the cargo being laid on top. This allowed for air circulation but also meant that any condensation on the metal decks wouldn't affect the cargo. Dunnage didn't last for many voyages before it became broken and useless for its task. We would take the broken bits up onto the deck and sling them overboard. Yes, we were litter louts. However, eventually the wood would be washed up somewhere and, no doubt, used for fuel. Another job supervised by the Chippy was caulking and pitching wooden decks. It was a dirty task but an essential one. After the old caulking had been scraped out, hemp or jute fibre impregnated with tar was pressed into the seams between deck planks. Of course, this was deemed to be just the job for cadets but members of the crew were roped in also.

At last, the prospect of shore leave for the first time since Antwerp. But, after a couple of weeks at sea, walking was odd at first – there was no motion to dry land. Bob plus Jim the Second Sparks and I set off for town. We wanted a coffee and we found just the place. Not only did it have coffee, but some amazing ice-cream concoctions as well. It was a 'Young Things' place with a juke box. Each four-person booth had its own selection box for the music. Coffee was ordered and we chose **our** music – Elvis Presley singing *Blue Suede Shoes*. This was our favourite painting song and we joined in quietly with Elvis. Soon other tables were joining in.

So we played it again and this time sang more loudly. Then someone from another table selected Elvis again but this time *I'm all Shook Up*. By now the whole café was in full song, not necessarily knowing all the words but certainly making a racket. And people were up and rocking away. We stayed in the café for a couple of hours and came out hoarse but thinking that Port Elizabeth was a great port. We had been nowhere except the café but to us it was a great town; unfortunately, it was time to report back to the ship. *Blue Suede Shoes* remained our favourite working song for the rest of the voyage – much to the annoyance of everyone else. Onwards to East London. We were allowed an evening ashore there and headed straight for the *Missions to Seamen* centre. Started by a Church of England padre in the nineteenth century, there are *Mission to Seafarers* (new name since my days at sea) clubs throughout the world. It's a non-profit charity and always provides a friendly welcome and a good meal at a fair price – an all-day breakfast was the favourite. There were games rooms with billiards and table-tennis tables and dart boards. Those needing counselling could find friendly advice and help. Also, from time to time they held dances. You always hoped that as the song said, "All the nice girls love a sailor"... but were usually disappointed. Feeling bloated on eggs, bacon, sausages, beans and chips it was time to return to the ship which was already flying the Blue Peter ("All aboard, vessel is about to proceed to sea.") Next stop Durban.

The approach to Durban could cause problems for ships of any size. There was often an ocean swell and a strong current. The harbour mouth was narrow with a headland on one side and a long mole on the other. You most certainly needed a local Pilot to take you in. I had sailed into the harbour once before – on the *Nevasa* with my family on our way back from Hong Kong to the UK. Durban was a lovely place and we were there for a few days. We went ashore but didn't do much apart from wander around and go to the cinema – in those days known locally as 'The Bio'. The Second Mate was engaged to a South African and this was to be his last voyage before emigrating. She came aboard for lunch. And someone else had a female cousin who also visited the ship. So we had two very good-looking young ladies at lunch with us. None of us were in a hurry to leave the dining room. But British Mercantile Marine vessels couldn't lie idle in harbour just because there were nice ladies on board. Soon we were on our way up the east coast towards Portuguese East Africa (now Mozambique).

Lourenço Marques (now Maputo) was our destination. It had been founded by one of Vasco da Gama's captains in the late fifteenth century. We off-loaded the last of our cargo and now were loading huge wooden crates full of tobacco. The dockers were very strong – they had to be to deal with the crates. They almost went into a trance as they did their work – moving in a kind of slow-motion dance and singing.

Odd to watch but very effective. When they took a break they fished over the side of the ship for a kind of catfish. They caught plenty.

With our cargo on board, it was time to sail for Beira farther up the coast. Beira, the second largest port, also acted as the main port for land-bound Rhodesia. It was quite a pleasant town but with nothing much for impecunious cadets to do. We became thirsty tramping around and stopped at a wayside stall where they were selling freshly crushed orange juice. The others didn't want any but I drank a glass – BIG MISTAKE! By the time we got back on board I wasn't feeling very well. I spent the rest of the day on the toilet and then found that anything I ate, even soup, wouldn't stay down. The Purser, who doubled up as a quasi-doctor, did his best with his medicines but it was clear that I had dysentery, hopefully a mild version. I wrote a letter to Mum announcing that I had dysentery and that it wasn't very nice. However I was quite proud of it as I could now claim another foul disease to go with the malaria I had caught as a small child in India, and all the rotten illnesses I caught when we returned to the UK from the Far East in 1949 – chicken pox, measles, mumps, asthma, rheumatic fever, glandular fever, etc. My letter went off in the mail sack. A little later the Captain called by to see how I was and to say that he had called for a shore doctor. Had I written to my parents? Yes, I had written to Mum.

"What did you tell her?"

"I told her I had dysentery."

He nearly went through the cabin bulkhead.

"Dowey lad, you are a minor and under my supervision. You shouldn't do that sort of thing! When your mother receives your letter she will be very worried about you. But by then you should be well into recovery. Alright, what I'll do in a day or two is see how you are and then send a radio message to Clan Line in UK. They can send your mother a telegram to update her. And that will be before she receives your letter. Dowey lad, as they say in your country – don't be such an eejit in future!"

Three or four days later I was over the worst of it but still didn't want to eat much. I wandered around looking like a large stick insect and had little strength, but after a while I got my appetite back. In the meantime, Clan Line had managed to get in touch with Mum before my letter arrived and told her that the dysentery flap was over. We had reached the end of our outward trip and now it was time to head for home.

We rounded the Cape of Good Hope and headed north. There was very little to see. Sometimes a passing ship but no land; the *Macleod* was making best speed for the Home Ports with full holds. Relations

DOWEY LAD GOES TO SEA
in the 50s

Star Ferry, Hong Kong Harbour

Hong Kong Harbour from The Peak

The newest cadet in the Merchant Navy

Carefully but Fearlessly

Clan Macleod

**Mum
Carrie
sports my cap**

**Dad
Major David Dowey
in Ghana**

Clan Macleod in dry dock

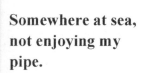

Somewhere at sea, not enjoying my pipe.

**Cargo dhow
Kakinada**

**Kakinada
fishermen**

**Colachel
diving boys.**

Bumboat in Aden

**The Gateway to
India
BOMBAY
Street Scene**

**Bombay Railway
Station**

Calcutta docks

Victoria Memorial Calcutta

**Working kit.
Second Leckie with Dowey lad.**

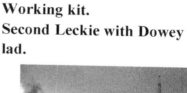

**Port Sudan
Tramp steamer loading goats**

with Ian, the Senior Cadet, hadn't got any better. We largely ignored each other (though that's rather difficult when you share a cabin) and talked only on work-related matters. To me he was a competent seaman but I noticed that the Navigating Officers had reservations about him. This became apparent when, on a beautiful Saturday afternoon as we ploughed northwards in the Atlantic on a flat calm sea, I was summoned to the bridge. The Captain and Chief Mate were there. Chief Mate:

"Dowey lad, we need you on the bridge in an hour's time to take the last two hours of my watch. I'll be with the Captain in his cabin. We'll be having a meeting. So get yourself up here for six o'clock. Get an early supper before you come up."

"Aye aye, sir." (Gulp.)

Back down to the cabin. Ian:

"What did the Mate want you for?"

"To take over the bridge at six for a couple of hours."

Ian was silent. As the senior, he should have been the one. Too bad.

Blimey. Better think this through. This is my first trip and I have so much still to learn about navigation and control of the bridge. Better skim through some text books. Better take a couple of them up with me.

The Chief Mate looked hard at me when I appeared on the bridge clutching a stack of my navigation manuals but made no comment.

"Right, Dowey lad. I'll be immediately below you

in the Captain's cabin, and you have instant access to me by the voice pipe. Use it if you need to but leave us in peace if you can. The Quartermaster has the course. Stay on it for the rest of the watch. See you at eight bells."

"Aye aye, sir."

Wow! In charge of a fully-laden merchant ship making 14 knots up the South Atlantic. Better do a bit of pacing (like the Mates do) and keep checking on the heading. Look into the radio cabin (part of the bridge) to say hello to the Second Sparks.

"You know why they're down in the Captain's Cabin, Derek?"

"Yes. They're having a meeting."

"Well, sort of. They're having a beer and listening to the UK sports results on the radio. We get good reception here."

We docked at Tilbury on the Thames and were then at the mercy of the dockers – they had a very powerful union in those days. Once the cargo for London had been unloaded, I was given the task of going down to one of the lower holds to deal with the tobacco casks for continental ports. I was to take a paint pot and a brush and label the casks 'A' for Antwerp. The others were for Rotterdam. So I took a cargo plan down and started painting. One of the older dockers approached me:

"You can't do that."

"Why not?"

"Because we call for a partly disabled docker to do that sort of thing. That's our agreement with the port authorities."

"How long will that take?"

"Three or four hours before he turns up."

"But we sail in four hours' time. I'll speak to the Mate."

The Mate told me that we would have to comply otherwise the blighters (my word, not his) would bring the whole dock out on strike. So we waited and waited for some old eejit to appear and paint under my instruction... and he used my brush and paint! The job took about fifteen minutes but, in the meantime, we had missed our tide and had to wait for the next one. The whole thing was ridiculous. However, we eventually got away and made a quick sortie across to Antwerp and Rotterdam to deliver their tobacco. After that, Manchester to drop more of it.

Manchester is approached through the Manchester Ship Canal. It's quite narrow with several locks. In those days you passed through dreary industrial areas and, given that this was a wet November in Lancashire, there was nothing to write home about. We eventually tied up in the Manchester docks and I skipped ashore to get papers for the Navigators. As usual, I turned first to the sports pages. What's this? Manchester United are at home to Tottenham Hotspur on Saturday! My team, the good old Spurs, would be playing here on Saturday and we wouldn't be sailing until Sunday! So three of us headed for Old Trafford that Saturday afternoon hoping that we would get in. These were two of the top teams in England so there would be a big crowd. Fortunately we did get in; the place was heaving. In those days most of the crowd stood for the whole match and so there would be more spectators than in the all-seater stadiums of today. This was the time of the 'Busby Babes'. Matt Busby (later 'Sir Matt') had put together a fine young team which played exciting football and was having a very successful season. Spurs were a classy side with some outstanding performers like Danny Blanchflower, the captain of Northern Ireland. His brother turned out for United that day. It was a tremendous match. I was already hoarse by half-time … Spurs were leading 4–1. Manchester came out in the second half determined to do something about that score line. Wave after wave of red shirts swept down the pitch and crashed on the Spurs goalmouth to the roars of the crowd. Manchester scored... 2–4. And again... 3–4. The crowd were going wild; the level of noise was amazing. All in vain... Spurs held on to their lead. I was completely drained of emotion. It had been surreal. For the first time in my life I had seen my lovely Spurs. And they had beaten one of the best teams in the land in a pulsating match. I had been there! Wow! I floated back to the *Macleod*.

"What are you smiling about, Dowey lad?"

"I've just watched Spurs beat United, sir."

"Is that right? Well, this will make you even more happy. We've just been told that our tobacco for Glasgow is to go to Belfast instead. You can sign off there and take some leave."

That damp November day turned out to be one of my best.

Soon the dear old *Macleod* delivered me to Belfast Docks. Then off by train to Omagh to be with Mum and brother Terence and some real home-cooking. (Dad was still serving in Ghana.) We had a pleasant Christmas but I can't remember much else about my leave – walked around my old haunts (we lived in Omagh in 1950–53 before we went to Hong Kong), met a few school friends and generally ate heartily and lazed around. The leave was soon over and it was time to head back to London to the *Macleod* which was loading for another deep sea voyage. Once back on board I heard the news... we're off to India. Wow! My birthplace. Bob was due back in a day or two but Ian had been assigned to another ship. The new arrangement of only two cadets was to work out fine – two's company, three's a crowd. But before Bob got back it was New Year's Eve and I had a duty to perform. By tradition, the youngest man on board rings the ship's bell on the stroke of midnight to welcome in the new year. So off I went to the bow of the ship and waited by the ship's bell for the Chief

Mate's call on the intercom. Eventually:

"Now, Dowey lad!"

So I rang the bell like crazy and youngsters did the same on all the ships in Tilbury Docks. Quite a racket. Then back to the dining room for my first beer – 1st January 1958. Oh yes, I had drunk shandy and cider before but this was my first beer.

Once Bob had returned we decided to take it in turns to be the 'Senior' Cadet. Bob would go one morning for briefing by the Chief Mate, I would go the next and so on. When any of the Mates were talking to one of us it was always:

"You and your mate will be on blah, blah, blah duties and…"

Never "Bob and you" or "Derek and you", but always "You and your mate". The only officer change for this trip was our new Second Mate, Rory. He was a super chap with a soft Hebridean accent. On joining the Merchant Marine he had decided not to do the usual four-year cadetship/apprenticeship but instead volunteered for four years 'before the mast', i.e. as an ordinary seaman. Rory said that he thought he would learn more about the nitty-gritty of shipboard work by doing that. Then, at the end of four years he went ashore for a couple of months to study for the Mates' exam. He passed easily and his first appointment as Third Mate had been on another Clan Line ship. Now we were fortunate to have him on the *Macleod*;

a great seaman and a fine chap. By now the ship was fully loaded so off we went – eastward ho!

But before turning east there was the southern run down the English Channel and the Bay of Biscay to negotiate. The Bay was in a foul mood and we were tossed and rolled about all the way through. And Bob and I now had the major problem of not having a third cadet on board: there were only two of us to do the watches on the bridge when the ship was in busy sea lanes. Four hours on the bridge and four off for days on end is not much fun. By the time we had cleared Gibraltar and were in the open Mediterranean, Bob and I were like zombies. Our super Chief Mate knew the remedy:

"Dowey lad, I don't want to see you or your mate on the bridge or doing any work for the next 48 hours."

Super Chief Mate, super idea. We slept for much of the time. I had been looking forward to sailing through the normally tranquil Mediterranean again. The last time I had been through it was on the *Empire Fowey* four years before on the way to Hong Kong. That time we had a virtually flat calm passage. This time was very different. The Med was worse than the Bay of Biscay. The waves were huge (I didn't stop to measure them!) and the *Macleod* was really chucked around. But the work of the ship had still to go on; our wretched job of taking the temperature of the holds twice a day was as important as ever – it would have been hair-raising work if our hair had not been plastered to our heads with sea water. Eventually we made Port Said at the north end of the Suez Canal. Phew!

Up until December 1956, as you sailed into the mouth of the canal at Port Said you passed a statue on the breakwater – Ferdinand de Lesseps. He was the Frenchman who had built the canal. But in '56 an Egyptian mob destroyed the statue in a fit of post-colonial pique. At Port Said, you rarely went alongside at a wharf but instead tied up to buoys to the side of the main waterway leading into the canal. You then waited for the next convoy to form up and for your Pilot to come aboard. The canal was not wide enough for two-way traffic so the northbound convoy had to come through before you could head south with yours. We waited. This gave the bumboatmen the opportunity to clamber on board and set out their wares. Some bumboatmen were almost 'by appointment' to Clan Line; these were the ones we trusted and so were allowed on board. Others had to be content to bob around in their boats alongside. The 'trusted' few had been coming aboard Clan ships for so long that they had adopted Scottish accents and had even given themselves Scottish names. One called himself Jock Mackay. They were an interesting bunch of cut-throats and only the unwary bought much from them. Then the Egyptian Pilot came on board and the convoy started to form up. We swung his small craft on board with its two-man crew. That's how he would return to shore once we got into the Red Sea.

"All bumboatmen ashore."

Then we were off at a steady six knots along with around twenty other ships. The speed was strictly controlled, partly to stop wear and tear on the canal sides. I loved sailing through the canal. I had already done so several times on troopships – *Strathnaver*, *Nea Hellas*, *Empire Halladale* and *Empire Fowey*. But this time I was on my own ship and I was on the bridge. I stayed up there for most of our passage, including telling Bob I would do two successive watches but would like breaks for meals. It was fascinating. On the west side a road ran parallel to the canal and across from it was a 'freshwater' canal which fed the farmers' fields. That canal was called the 'Sweetwater' Canal in the British times, because it was semi-stagnant and stank. To the east there was no road, no water, no greenery, just desert. The exceptions were an isolated village or two. But it wasn't canal all the way to the Red Sea. There were three salt lakes to pass through – Lake Timsah, the Great Bitter Lake and the Little Bitter Lake. Sometimes convoys had to tie up to buoys in the lakes to allow other convoys to come through.

I read some years later that the handover of Pilot duties from the international Pilots to Egyptian Pilots in 1956 had been smooth and that the Egyptian Pilots were very competent. Well, some of them may have been but I know of one who certainly wasn't. The journey of a convoy takes around fifteen hours. Ours left Port Said just after midnight. We were plodding steadily along with our 'Suez light' showing the way; it was a searchlight which the Canal Authorities required us to set up on the forecastle. We were keeping careful eyes on the Russian oil tanker ahead of us. Suddenly her lights looked different. She had swung sideways and appeared to have run into the canal bank. Worse... we were closing on her. Our Egyptian Pilot didn't have a clue what to do but fortunately, our super Chief Mate was on the bridge and took command:

"Dead slow engines!"

"Dead slow it is, sir!"

"Emergency lights fore and aft!"

"Emergency lights it is, sir!"

Both Bob and I were on the bridge.

"Moore lad! Wake the Third Mate and tell him to rouse the port watch and get a boat over on the port side and await orders."

"Wake the Third Mate, port watch to get a boat over the port side and await orders it is, sir!" And Bob shot off.

We were still closing on the tanker.

"Engines slow astern!"

"Engines slow astern it is, sir!"

"Keep your heading, Secuni!"

"Keeping my head, sahib!"

"Dowey lad! Roust out the starboard watch. One half to go for'ard, one aft, each to ready cables for tying up!"

"Starboard watch, half forward, half aft, cables ready for tying up sir!" And I was away.

Anyway, by careful handling of the rudder and the engines, the Chief Mate kept us in mid-stream short of the tanker. Fortunately, the ships behind us knew there was an emergency (we were in radio contact and they had seen our emergency lights) and all slowed down then stopped. (So we didn't have a re-enactment of the Disney film scene in *Jungle Book* when a line of elephants all crashed into the next one when the lead elephant stopped! The Disney film scene would have been tame stuff if our convoy had crashed into us.) But we had the Man of the Moment in our Chief Mate. And the Third Mate and his crew did great work in the lifeboat getting the cables onto the buoys. Phew! And what had the Pilot been doing all this time? Flapping around like a headless chicken and getting in the way generally. Our Chief Mate knew everything about the ship and how to deal with crises. In an emergency, I imagine that he would even have been able to do something useful in the engine room. There wasn't much he hadn't seen or done at sea. And he was a survivor... he had been torpedoed twice in the Atlantic during World War Two. Finally we were through the canal and cleared away from Port Suez. Our incompetent Pilot was dropped (with his crew in his boat!) and we headed out into the open sea – the Red Sea, so-called apparently because of the red algae which sometimes appears. I remember only one incident as we sailed along. It was about shoes.

The working shoes that our Cabin Steward had found for me when I first signed on were now falling apart. But on my last leave I had sorted out the shoe situation and had stowed an old but serviceable pair in my sea-trunk. When you discarded anything (shirts, caps, shoes, etc.) you usually left them on the deck behind the accommodation superstructure. The deck sweepers would leave them there to give the crew a chance to pick them up and get some more wear out of them. So I placed the beaten-up shoes on the deck. They must have been really decrepit as they stayed there for a couple of days with no takers. Finally I watched one of the sweepers pick them up and chuck them over the side. Those shoes were real old Sea Dogs and it was fitting that they had been committed to the deep.

The rest of the passage down the Red Sea was uneventful and we reached Aden to take on engine fuel. In every port, a ship had a shipping agent. He was relied on to arrange a berth or a buoy, ensure refuelling, make any cargo arrangements and generally make a ship's stay as short as possible – port charges were usually high. A ship was only financially efficient when it was bowling along at sea with a full cargo and heading for its discharging port. We tied up to a buoy in Aden harbour and then were at the mercy of the shipping agent and the port authorities. The ship was surrounded by bumboats and swimmers diving for coins but all went well and we were soon on our way again. (Aden town and the surrounding area had few attractions as I had previously found out when going ashore from a troopship. And anyway we weren't granted shore leave.) We headed out into the Arabian Sea. Next port Bombay – the 'Gateway to India'.

The last time I had been in Bombay (now called Mumbai) was aged six when Dad had come down from Lahore to meet Mum and me on our return to India from Ireland. The port was the busiest in India and, by golly, it certainly was busy. We went alongside and, as there was a lot of cargo to discharge and some to take on, we had time for half a day ashore. But before doing that we had to deal with the various vendors who had come on board. I was measured for a couple of shirts which were promised for the following day (and duly arrived), and I handed over a couple of my favourite books to be rebound in leather (he did a very good job). Then it was time to head ashore with Bob and Jim, the Second Radio Officer. As we left the dock gates, a hawker latched on to us.

"You buy pens, pencils, notebooks from me, very cheap."

"No, thank you,"

"I get you anything you want Bombay."

"No, we just want to walk around."

"I show you everywhere."

"No thank you."

He tailed us for quite some time, gradually reducing his prices on his pens, pencils, etc. but we didn't buy a thing from him. Well, he didn't have anything we wanted. We wandered around Bombay taking in the sights, sounds and aromas, some nice and some not. Bob and Jim were amazed at the sight of cattle lying down in the middle of the road, wandering into shops or browsing serenely on some unfortunate's fruit stall. The Hindus regard them as sacred so the cattle did what they wanted. Everywhere there was hustle and bustle (apart from the cattle). Many people in Bombay were simply trying to earn enough money to feed their families that day. Tomorrow would be the same. There certainly was a lot of poverty with many people literally living on the streets, but most seemed cheerful and just got on with life as best they could.

Of course we also had work to do in port. Our ship had five holds and each had three levels... upper hold, 'tween decks and lower hold. One afternoon I was down in one of the lower holds, stripped to the waist with the sweat dripping off me. A diagram of the required stowage of cargo was in my hand and I was directing a motley group of Indian dockers as to where to stow it as it came swinging down in cargo nets.

A voice from up top:

"Derek! Derek!"

I wasn't in the best of moods having been down in the hold in the damp heat for a couple of hours.

"Yes! What is it?"

"Do you remember the Spurs match in Manchester in November?"

What sort of question was that when I'm down in this smelly hold supervising cargo stowage?

"Yes, of course I do. What about it?"

"Well, we've just heard on the radio that a plane carrying the United team has crashed in Germany! Some have been killed and others injured!"

It was terrible news. We learned later that 23 lives had been lost including eight of the United team. Etched firmly in my memory is the date of the crash – 6th February 1958 – and where I heard the news.

From Bombay we headed south along the Malabar coast and visited two ports. Some ports are truly memorable; Cochin was one. It had been an important port for hundreds of years and was one of the first to do trade with Western countries; the Portuguese were the first of many. As you approached you saw a coast lined with beaches and cocoa-nut palms; and here and there was a creek leading inland. Beyond them, the town was red and white – white buildings with red-tiled roofs. And all around you would be fishing boats. We had arranged to play another Clan ship at football here and were keenly looking forward to it. Unfortunately, the other ship was re-routed. Neither Bob nor I managed to get ashore as we were on cargo supervision throughout our stay. Then we sailed south to the next port of call – Colachel, virtually at the extreme south of India. It was first used for trading with Western nations by the Danes (yes, believe it or not!) then the Dutch and eventually by the British. As soon as you anchored you were surrounded by small canoes sculled along by diving boys. The sculls were simply split bamboos. The boys yelled up that they would dive for coins and so they did. Having loaded copra, it was time to move on from the west coast (the Malabar) to the east (the Coromandel). We sailed south, rounded Ceylon and headed north. There were four ports to call at on the Coromandel, the first being Madras (now Chennai).

A little over ten years before, as a wee lad of seven, the British were leaving India and I had sailed with my father's regiment from Madras bound for Hong Kong. Madras was a busy place but not as busy as Bombay. The people were different… very dark and more laid-back than the Bombay folk. In our short run ashore, what I remember best was the 'optician'. This was a chap who was sitting at the side of the road with a couple of baskets. In one was a motley collection of second-hand spectacle frames; in the other was a pile of lenses. A customer would rummage through the lenses basket to find what suited him. Then he would try them in various frames. After that, a squint at a chart showing different sizes of letters. If he was satisfied, the 'optician' would fix the lenses into frames using a small pot of glue. Money given, money received, next customer. Everyone happy, hopefully. That's my abiding memory of Madras. We cleared away for several smaller ports.

As we approached Kakinada, I was perched on the small platform at the bottom of a gangway which had been lowered over the side. I was 'sounding' the depth of water under the ship as we cautiously approached land. I had a piece of ancient technology in my hands... a rope with pieces of coloured cloth at intervals and with a heavy lead weight at the end. The cloth markers were equally placed on the rope and showed fathoms (roughly six feet). The idea was to swing the lead forward and let go so that it was on the bottom when you passed directly over it. You watched for the cloth markers and yelled out the depth of water below. Then you hauled up the lead and swung it again:

"By the mark!" you shouted... and then perhaps, "Seven!" and so on.

(Sailors thought that swinging the lead was a good easy job to do, so the saying 'swinging the lead' came in to the English language to mean 'avoiding hard work'.)

I was indeed literally 'swinging the lead'.

When the Captain felt he was as close as he dared, he ordered the anchor to be dropped. So we swung at anchor off this idyllic little 'port' – less a port more a strip of sand with huts and palm trees beyond – Kakinada. Within minutes of anchoring, wooden craft set off from shore towards us. The larger vessels contained our cargo – copra. These boats were all under sail although they had auxiliary engines for manoeuvring and for emergencies. So for most of the day we had craft tied to our side with our derricks working away swinging the copra in sacks on board. Meantime, other sailing vessels came out. These were fishing boats and their crews had fish for sale. We bought quite a lot for the mess and the crew also bought from them. The favourites were prawns and barracuda.

But the most interesting craft were the canoes. These were more rudimentary than those we had seen at Colachel. They were made of three slim palm trunks lashed together. When you were on them you were continually wet as you rode them like a horse with your legs underwater. Some boats had small outriggers for stability. As at Colachel, the sculls were lengths of split bamboo. Each canoe would have two or three young lads sitting astride them skylarking and laughing and diving for coins; it looked like good fun. So the Second Sparks and I put on swimming trunks, zipped a few rupees in the pockets, and went over the side to have a go. We were each hauled on to a canoe, handed a paddle and off we went. There was a race to the shore. What a noise as we shouted and laughed and tried to knock other crews overboard. Soon we hit the beach. After strolling around for a while we held up some rupees and told our 'crews' we would pay them when we got back to the ship. So there was another mad race back. The crews were paid off and we scrambled up the companion-way laughing and joking. To be met at the top by:

"Dowey lad. Report to the Captain. Now."

Captain Sahib was not in a good mood. He informed me that I was still a minor and, as such, I was in his charge.

"Dowey lad, did you know that barracuda frequent these waters?" Yes I did. We had bought some from the fishermen.

"Do you know what barracuda can do to people swimming in the water or dangling their legs off canoes? Especially white legs?"

No, I didn't.

"Well, let me tell you, Dowey lad. Two or three years ago a Clan ship came to this very port and a cadet went over the side and messed around on a canoe just as you did. He was attacked by a barracuda that savaged one leg so badly that they had to amputate it!"

Blimey!

"We were yelling at you as soon as you went in but you were shouting and laughing, and mustn't have heard us."

"No I certainly didn't hear you, sir."

"Well, lad. Don't be so damn stupid again. Think, and seek permission. Go and see the Chief Mate. He has something to say to you."

He certainly did. He went over it all again. And I got four hours extra cargo-stowing duties.

Big eejit!

Eventually, with our consignment safely stowed away, we weighed anchor and headed for Visakhapatnam. (Just to mention that in World War Two Kakinada was the beach where British and Indian troops practised assaults in landing craft in preparation for a beach landing on Japanese-held Burma.)

Visakhapatnam or Vizag (as it was known to the cognoscenti of the Merchant Marine) was (again according to the cognoscenti) the arsehole of the world. It had a narrow, dirty little estuary and a miserable dockland. Even worse, it had the unenviable reputation of being the easiest place to catch venereal disease anywhere in the world.

"Dowey lad. If you go ashore, you stay clear of them women. Otherwise you'll end up with the clap. I remember a fellow who went to a brothel here, then later got married to a nice girl back in the UK and infected not only his new wife but the wee baby they had later. I remember another bloke who went ashore here and a month or two later his John Thomas fell off. Then there was another..."

"Stop! Stop! Enough! I'm not going ashore."

Thankfully we weren't in Vizag for very long, and were soon on our way to Calcutta via another little port called Bhimunipatnam (much the same as Kakinada but no canoeing for Dowey lad!). Calcutta was a very busy port. It was sixty or so miles from the sea up the Hooghly River. You couldn't simply pop in to Calcutta, load/unload and be on your way. No. You had to wait your turn. You anchored in the estuary in the Bay of Bengal and waited for two things... an empty berth/buoy in the port and, of course, a Pilot; they both had to become available at the same time. We were quite lucky – we spent only one week out in the Bay. But it was a long week and people got dispirited and touchy. When a ship is alive and at sea that's the best time. The next best time is when you are loading/unloading in port and have a chance to go ashore. And the worst time by far is languishing out at anchor waiting to go in. I heard of ships which, for various reasons had to swing at anchor for up to three months at the mouth of the Hooghly awaiting their turn.

I came to a big decision out there at anchor. It was simple: you don't have to smoke a pipe to be a Sea

Dog. There were people on board who were perfectly good Sea Dogs who didn't smoke. I had to admit to myself that, although I had tried very hard to enjoy pipe smoking, I didn't. I didn't like the taste, and the smoke made me cough and made my eyes stream. As I leaned on a rail staring out at the dirty brown sea, with my pipe in my hand, I made my big decision. I chucked the pipe into the Bay of Bengal. Then I went off to my cabin to collect the remains of the large packet of tobacco bought in Antwerp.

I know who would like this – George, the Second Electrician (Second Lecky in seaboard slang) – he smokes a pipe.

"George, it's your lucky day. I've given up the pipe. I've decided I don't like smoking so you can have my remaining tobacco."

"That's very kind of you, Derek. Let's have a look at it. Well now. This is interesting. You've been smoking this in your pipe since when?"

"Since Antwerp, middle of last year."

"And you don't like it."

"That's right. I gave it a good go, but I have to admit that I've never liked it. I thought I would eventually."

"Well, pipe tobacco should be slow-burning and good pipe tobacco is not harsh on your throat."

"Yes maybe, but this stuff was very harsh indeed."

"Indeed it would be. That's because this isn't pipe tobacco. This is cigarette tobacco. No wonder you didn't enjoy it. This sort of stuff burns like a wee volcano in your pipe bowl. So thanks for thinking of me but it's no good to me."

So I took the stuff to someone who rolled his own cigarettes. And that was the end of my smoking... tobacco ceased to be on my agenda from that day to this.

At anchor there is still work to do on board ship but there is also time to relax and to talk. I had been giving a lot of thought to my future. I was really enjoying my time at sea and was looking forward to eventually being a Third Mate and working my way on up the ladder. But several of the officers – navigators and engineers – had told me that one really needed to make a decision early in one's time at sea. They were almost all of the same opinion – it was a good life for ten years or so but then most people wanted to go ashore. By then you would be married or you wanted to marry; spending three to six months or even more away became more and more difficult for you. And, if you left the Merchant Navy, what job would you do? Well, some people managed to get employment on the passenger ferries to France and Ireland etc. but there were only a limited number of those jobs. So what else could one do with one's Certificate in Navigation? Well, that was a good question.

"And don't forget, Dowey lad, that if you fail your regular eyesight tests that will be the end of your career as a Navigator."

"But what about if you got fitted with spectacles?"

"No. You do your test without spectacles. They're strict about that."

"Blimey. But people's eyesight gets worse gradually."

"Correct. But the Merchant Navy has its rules."

I also chatted to the Chief Mate and to the Captain and told them that I was thinking of going ashore and joining the Army. They gave me similar advice – if I had any doubts about a career at sea, now was the time to make the decision. They thought I could do well at sea but also saw no reason why I couldn't have a good career in the Army. I mulled over the advice. Eventually the decision was to go ashore and join the Army. So, two big decisions were made while at anchor in the Bay of Bengal – first to throw my pipe into it, and second to join the Army. Letters were prepared to go off to Mum in Omagh and Dad in Ghana to tell them the news.

Eventually the *Macleod* was called forward, a Pilot appeared and we made our way up the Hooghly. It's a treacherous waterway as the channels keep changing due to the flood waters of the Ganges. Eventually we tied up on buoys fore and aft in mid-stream at Calcutta and awaited our time to go into the docks. The Hooghly/Ganges was muddy brown. All sorts of rubbish floated downstream past us towards the sea – fruit, tree branches, household rubbish, dead animals and sometimes dead humans; the Ganges was the sacred Hindu river and cremated ashes and partly cremated bodies were often committed to it.

"Dowey lad, are you going ashore with your mate?"

"We hope to, sir."

"Well, you've seen the state of the river. Mind yourself getting on and off the water taxi. If you fall in you're bound to swallow some water and then it will be off to a hospital to be pumped out and then a long course of injections. Not a pleasant experience. And we'll sail without you."

"I'll be careful, sir."

Bob and I did go ashore for an afternoon and wandered around a bit. Hawkers and shopkeepers alike attempted to get us to buy something but, on two pounds a week, we weren't good customers. Some of the streets with covered walkways had become residential areas – there were makeshift homes all along them. Cardboard, corrugated iron sheets and rattan mats had been fashioned into little homes. Everywhere there were small children gambolling about as their mothers washed clothes in buckets and did the cooking. Strangely, in this abject poverty, most people seemed to be in good humour. Back to the ship. Once we got into the docks, unloading and loading was completed quickly and we were soon on our way on a fairly long leg of our journey: Calcutta to Port Sudan.

After a couple of days at sea I was looking around the cabin for my wallet; not for any reason other than I didn't know where it was. I remembered that I had had it ashore with me in Calcutta and, indeed, that I had taken it out of my pocket to pay the water-boatman who took us back to the ship. I couldn't believe that I had dropped it in his boat. So surely it had reached the cabin with me. But where was it? When returning from shore I had the habit of chucking the wallet on the writing desk which Bob and I shared. But it wasn't there. I hunted high and low and Bob did too. No wallet. I asked the Cabin Steward if he had seen it. No, he hadn't. I began to suspect him but what should I do? Ask the Chief Mate if the steward's belongings could be searched? But that didn't sound sensible. Surely, if he had stolen it he would have taken the money (five pounds sterling and some Indian rupees) and got rid of the wallet. So I did nothing except be rather cool to the Cabin Steward for a few days. Once shipboard routine had settled down and we were on top of our work the Chief Mate told us it was time we painted our cabin. We reckoned we were pretty good painters by now having tackled all sorts of painting jobs around the ship – the Flying Bridge, the library, the sick bay, the lifeboats, etc... the sort of places where the crew were not trusted to do a good job. So now we set-to on our cabin. First of all take out all belongings and store them in an empty cabin. Then unscrew everything and lay it out on deck (ship's furniture, beds, lockers, etc. are all screwed down). And when we had unscrewed the writing desk, what did we find lying behind it? Good guess. The missing wallet. Rejoice like the lady in the Bible finding the missing talent! And, because I had wrongly suspected him (but never accused him), I gave the Cabin Steward a generous half-journey tip.

What on earth could there be to load in Port Sudan? Surely the Sudan is a desert country. Well, indeed there is a lot of desert but the Nile River flows right through the country and, apart from other produce, a lot of cotton is grown in its valley. Lancashire was a great exporter of cotton goods in those days and the mills needed the raw material. So that's what we loaded, bales of cotton. Each bale needed two dockers with billhooks. The dockers were Sudanese, they were very lean men but astonishingly strong. Unfortunately, they used camel urine to wash their hair. Why? Perhaps because water was so scarce? I don't know. What I did know was that supervising the loading of cotton bales in the lower hold, and breathing the stench of sweat and camel dung was not a pleasant experience. There was a tradition among the dockers. When a ship had almost finished loading, the acknowledged strongest man would be loaded with a cotton bale by his mates. He would then stagger up the companion-ways unaided all the way to the bridge, finally dropping the bale at the Captain's feet. This entitled him to a good reward for himself and his mates. Later, four (yes, four) of our seamen were required to haul that cotton bale away to the hold.

While we were in Port Sudan, our fine old Sea Dog the Chief Mate decided to check on the seaworthiness of our lifeboats. Looking after the lifeboats was one of the main responsibilities of the cadets. We had to ensure that they always looked good but, more importantly, that all their gear was serviceable, rations and water up to scale, etc. And, of course, our survivor of two sinkings during World War Two knew all about the value of lifeboats. He wanted to ensure that the lowering gear was in good order and that everything about the lifeboats was as required. Also, the crews needed practice in lowering the boats and handling them. Perhaps other Chief Mates quietly neglect to do all this but not our superman. As our full-scale lifeboat practice went ahead, you could see that crews on other ships in dock were leaning on their rails and watching us critically. But we had a good crew and they did their work well. The *Macleod* showed the other ships what a professional crew could do.

The voyage home via the Suez Canal and the Mediterranean was uneventful. These were my last days on the lovely *Macleod* and of course I was sad that I would not sail on her or any other Clan ship again. And I would miss my friends, in particular, Bob my mate, Jim the Second Radio Officer, Gus the Carpenter, Rory the Second Mate, Richard the Third, George the Second Lecky and, of course, my

Number One Seaman the Chief Mate. But I was also excited about becoming a soldier and following my father into the Royal Inniskilling Fusiliers. I had been born into the Regiment and had spent my childhood 'following the flag' with my parents. It was time to don khaki myself. But there was one more hurdle: the English Channel. We made our way up the busiest seaway in the world very warily as there was thick fog. Four knots was the maximum we could risk as, from the bridge, we couldn't see much farther than the bow. Two lookouts were up on the bow ready to ring the bell if they saw anything. Up on the bridge were the Second Mate, the Quartermaster, we two cadets and an extra lookout in each wing. In addition, the Captain and Chief Mate stalked around. Our radar was on but it wasn't very effective. At minute intervals a member of the crew sounded our mournful fog horn. And so did the other ships blundering around in the vicinity. I was out on one wing of the bridge when I thought I heard a fog horn astern of us so I called the Second Mate out to listen:

"Yes, I can hear it. Let's listen for the next fog horn. There it goes again. Dammit, it's getting closer. Listen again."

We waited.

"That's it again. It's coming up behind us fast. Dowey lad, get a look out on the stern to ring the bell if he sees her."

"Look out on the stern, ring the bell if he sees her it is, sir."

I briefed one of the wing look outs and he galloped off.

Seconds later we heard the mystery ship's horn loud and clear and there it was coming out of the fog... ahead of us! Passing parallel about fifty yards away! *What the hell?!* Yes, that's what happened. Noise can get distorted in fog. We reckoned that the mystery ship's fog horn calls were being bounced back from the superstructure behind our bridge, so that we on the wing thought the noise was coming from behind us. Very odd, and we were all mistaken. If the two ships had collided at the combined speed of around eight knots our super Chief Mate would almost certainly have notched up his third shipwreck. Eventually we cleared the fog and swung into the Thames Estuary. As usual with Clan ships with cargo for London, we tied up in Tilbury Docks. The docks are on the north side of the river opposite Gravesend which was a well-known haunt of seafarers and was reputed to have a pub for each day of the year.

"Dowey lad, you're leaving us tomorrow so what are you doing tonight?"

"I'm going up to London with the Third Engineer, sir. We'll listen to some jazz at Ronnie Scott's."

"Your last night in the Merchant Navy and you'll listen to jazz? You'll certainly not do that! You're coming ashore with us tonight to Gravesend."

So that evening five or six of us took the ferry across to Gravesend. Someone knew of a good pub and we spent the evening there recounting stories of our last and other voyages. This is what Sea Dogs did and I felt that, pipe or no pipe, I was now a Sea Dog. They plied me with drinks and we were all very merry. I was feeling great and all was fine until I needed to get off my stool and head for the toilet.

"Just going to the toilet."

I got off the stool, stood, tried to walk and instead fell flat on the floor. Roars of laughter.

"Dowey lad, you'll have to come back to sea! You haven't got land legs!"

Eventually it was time to leave and we all staggered down to the ferry, everyone holding on to someone else and laughing and shouting. On boarding the ferry:

"You need to stay out in the fresh air, Dowey lad, so we'll all go up onto the open deck."

I needed to pee again so I staggered away from the others to the aft end of the open deck and peed. There was a shriek from below,

"What the hell! Who's pissing up there!?"

People were sheltering on a small deck below me out of the wind.

My mates rallied around and hustled me away before any of the indignant (and damp) lot could get up the companion-way and find me.

The next day I signed off formally and collected my wages. Farewells were said and we all promised to write to each other. Chief Mate:

"Well, Dowey lad or, more correctly, Fusilier Dowey. You'll be welcome back if you don't like the Army. All the best to you and remember to beware of barracudas… be they fish-like or in human form!"

"Aye aye sir."

Bob accompanied me to the station in a taxi and helped me on to a train with my luggage. He waved me away. That was the end of my service in the Merchant Navy. Had it been worth it? Absolutely.

Postscript

MV *Clan Macleod*

The *Macleod* was built by the Greenock Dockyard Company in the Clyde in 1948.

Gross weight: 6,073 tons

Length	466 feet
Breadth	61 feet
Draught	38 feet

Sold to Alligator Shipping Co Ltd (Cyprus) in 1976. Scrapped at Gadani Beach, Pakistan in 1978.

Clan Line

Clan Line was formed in 1877 and later arranged trading alliances with other shipping companies such as King Line, Hector's and Bowaters. Crews were interchanged between the companies.

Then, in the late 1950s there was a major merger with the Union Castle Line. Each line kept its own name but the trading company became the British and Commonwealth Shipping Company. Clan Line itself finally ceased operations in 1981.

The song 'Farewell to the Clan Line' was written by Ron Baxter and set to music by Ross Campbell. The full version is at mudcat.org. Here are the first verse and the chorus:

Farewell to the Clan Line

When I think of the years that I spent a-sailing,
The thoughts of past times they drift back to me;
The dangers, the choices, the mayhem, the boredom,
The tears and the laughter, the sky and the sea.

Chorus
But those times are all gone by and so are the vessels;
The House Flag's been lowered for the very last time.
It's "Farewell" to Hector's and Union Castle,
To King and Bowater's and to the Clan Line.

Printed in Great Britain
by Amazon

68584621R10047